Scottish

A Wee Book of Clean

Compiled by Hugh Morrison

McNab had just won the lottery. He ordered a pint of 'heavy' in a pub to celebrate.

'That'll be £2.97,' said the barman.

McNab handed over three pounds. The barman poured the pint and put the change down on the bar.

'Have one yourself,' said McNab, feeling generous.

'Thanks very much, I'll take a double whisky,' replied the surprised barman.

A look of horror crossed McNab's face as he pointed to the bar.

'I meant one of the pennies!'

*

What do you call a Scottish dog lead?

McLeish.

*

Robert Burns was speaking to his publisher.

'It's no good,' said the poet. 'I cannot think of any words that will rhyme in my new poem.'

'Och, I keep telling ye, Rab,' said the canny businessman, 'if ye cannae think of a word, just make one up. Ye've done it in all your other poems and naebody's noticed so far!'

*

McTavish was on holiday in New York, and took a tour of the Empire State Building. At the top he asked what the wire mesh was for above the balcony rail.

'That's for safety reasons,' said the guide. 'Somebody threw a one cent coin off here recently and it shattered a car windscreen on the street below, causing the young couple in the car to have a fatal accident. It was such a tragic waste.'

'Aye, it must have been,' sighed McTavish. 'And it was a shame about that young couple dyin' as well.'

*

How many Scotsmen does it take to change a light bulb?

Och! It's no that dark!

*

'Come quickly doctor! Sandy's just got dragged under a tractor by his clothing!'

'Kilt?'

'Not quite, but he's badly injured.'

*

Two years after marriage, McTavish's wife asked for some money to buy a new dress, but he demanded to know why she needed one.

'Because,' she explained, 'I'm tired of people throwing confetti at me when I go shopping.'

*

How many Presbyterians does it take to change a lightbulb?

100. One to change the lightbulb, and the other 99 to walk out in disgust about changes to the kirk.

*

Sipping his whisky at home, Jamesie was advising his young son on responsible drinking.

'I always know ma limit. Ye see thae two glasses on theer?' said the father, pointing to the kitchen table. 'If ah thought ah could see *four* glasses theer, ah'd know it was time tae stop drinkin.'

'But pa,' objected the boy, 'there's only one glass there.'

*

'How's the house you're living in in London, son?' asked Sandy's mother when he phoned home to Inverness.

'Och it's no so bad,' he replied, 'but the woman next door keeps shouting and crying all night and the man on the other side keeps banging his head on the wall.'

'Never you mind,' said his mother, 'don't let them get to you, just you ignore them.'

'Aye, that I do,' said Sandy, 'I just keep on playing my bagpipes.'

*

'I've seen better days, sir,' said a tramp to an Aberdonian.

He replied, 'So have I – but I havna' time to discuss the weather the noo.'

*

'If I ever win the lottery, ah'm gonnae make sure my neighbours are rich too.'

'That's awfy kind of you tae remember that poor family next door.'

'Ah'm no givvin them anything. I'll be moving somewhere where everyone else is rich!'

*

A visitor to a small Scottish town which had four churches, none of which were well attended, asked an elder of one dying congregation, 'How's your church getting on?' 'Not very well', he said, 'but, thank the Lord, the others are no' doing any better.'

*

After discovering that they had won 10 million pounds in the lottery, McTavish and his wife sat down to discuss their future. Mrs McTavish announced:

'After twenty years of washing other people's stairs, I can throw my old scrubbing brush away at last.'

McTavish nodded in agreement.

'Of course ye can, dear. We can easily afford tae buy ye a new one now.'

McNab was almost in tears as he met McPherson in the street.

'My beautiful wee comb. I broke a tooth off it an' now I cannae use it anymore. What am I going to do? Now I'll have to buy another one.'

'Well,' said his friend, 'you don't need to buy another comb just because you lost one tooth off it.'

'But ye dinnae understand,' said McNab. 'It was the last tooth.'

*

McTavish was observed stripping the wallpaper from his front room.

'Redecorating?' asked a neighbour.

'No, moving house.'

*

Instead of his usual donation of a penny, McTavish accidentally put a ten pence piece in the collection plate at the kirk one Sunday.

The steward noticed the mistake, and in silence he passed by McTavish without offering the plate to him for nine more Sundays.

On the tenth Sunday, McTavish ignored the plate as usual, but the steward this time announced in a loud voice:

'Yer time's up, McTavish.'

*

McDougal asked the bus driver how much it would cost to travel into the centre of Glasgow.

'A poond' said the driver.

McDougal was shocked and decided to run after the bus for a few stops.

'How much noo?' he asked, after the doors hissed open.

'Still a poond'.

McDougal ran after the bus for another three stops and, panting, he asked

'How much noo?'

The driver smiled and replied: 'one poond fifty. Ye're runnin' the wrang way!'

*

An Edinburgh man visited the highlands and wasn't impressed by the size of the mountains.

'What's so great about them?' asked the southerner of a local farmer. 'I could climb that one in a day,' he said, pointing to the rising peak ahead of him on the path.

'I don't know aboot that' responded the farmer, 'a young couple went up this path last year and never came back.'

The Edinburghian suddenly looked fearful. 'Oh! Were they lost?'

'Naw,' was the reply, 'they went doon the other side!'

*

McNab was passing through a small highland town and knocked on the door of the manse.

'Minister, ye did me a favour ten years ago,' said McNab, 'and I have nivver forgotten it.'

'Ah,' replied the clergyman with a holy expression on his face, 'as the good book says, "there is more joy in heaven over one sinner that repenteth" – you've come back to repay me?'

'Not exactly,' replied McNab. 'I've just got into toon and need another favour, and I thought of you right away.'

*

McTavish: 'An' so ye leave Glesga' on Monday. What are ye daein' the morrow nicht?'

McDougal: 'Tomorrow, Thursday, I've no plans.'

McTavish: 'An' the next nicht?'

McDougal: 'I'm free then, too.'

McTavish: 'An' what will ye be daein on the Saturday?'

McDougal: 'On Saturday ah'm havin' dinner wi' the McPhersons.'

McTavish: 'What a pity! Ah wanted ye to take dinner wi'us on Saturday!'

*

Two drunks were taken to Glasgow General Hospital by a chip shop owner. One had a terribly burnt hand and the other was clutching his stomach and moaning.

'What's going on here?' asked the doctor, unable to get an answer from the men.

'It's like this, doc,' said the chippy owner. 'This one was payin' for his chips, but his wallet dropped in the batter. He grabbed it out but then it fell intae the deep fat fryer. He burnt his hond badly getttin' it oot, and then while I was helping him the other feller came in and ate the wallet.'

*

Two old Scotsmen sat by the roadside, talking and puffing away merrily at their pipes.

'There's no much pleasure in smokin' these days, Sandy,' said Donald.

'Hoo dae ye mak' that oot?' questioned Sandy.

'Weel,' said Donald, 'ye see, if ye're smokin' yer ain bacca ye're thinkin' o' the awfu' expense, an' if ye're smokin' some ither body's, yer pipe's packed sae tight it willnae draw.'

*

A Scotsman had been presented with a pint bottle of rare old Scotch whisky. He was walking briskly along the road toward home, when along came a car which he did not side step quite in time. It threw him down and hurt his leg quite badly. He got up and limped down the road. Suddenly he noticed that something warm and wet was trickling down his leg.

'Oh, God,' he groaned, 'I hope that's blood!'

*

A newly appointed Scots minister on his first Sunday of office had reason to complain of the poorness of the collection.

'Mon,' replied one of the elders, 'they are close, verra close.'

'But,' confidentially, 'the auld meenister he put three or four pennies intae the plate hissel', just to gie them a start. Of course he took the pennies awa' with him afterward.'

The new minister tried the same plan, but the next Sunday he again had to report a dismal failure. The total collection was not only small, but he was grieved to find that his own pennies were missing.

'Ye may be a better preacher than the auld meenister,' exclaimed the elder, 'but if ye had half the knowledge o' the world, an' o' yer ain flock in particular, ye'd ha' done what he did an' glued the pennies tae the plate.'

*

Sandy McDougal sat with his girlfriend Maggie on the sofa.

'A penny for your thoughts, Sandy,' murmured Maggie, after a silence of an hour and a half.

'Weel,' replied Sandy slowly, with surprising boldness, 'tae tell ye the truth, I was jist thinkin' how fine it wad be if ye were tae gie me a wee kiss.'

'I've nae objection,' simpered Maggie, and kissed him.

Sandy relapsed into a brown study once more, and the clock ticked twenty-seven minutes.

'An' what are ye thinkin' about noo; anither, eh?'

'Nae, nae, lassie; it's a mair serious matter ah'm thinking of the noo.'

'Is it, laddie?' asked Maggie softly. Her heart was going pit-a-pat with expectation.

'An' what might it be?'

'I was jist thinkin',' answered Sandy, 'that it was aboot time ye were paying me that penny!

*

After the defeat of Gordon Brown in the 2010 election, two Scotsmen were discussing politics in the pub.

Jamesie sighed. 'Aye, it's jist as I expected. We've only had a Tory prime minister for a few hours, and already a Scotsman's lost his hoose and his job.'

*

In the Western Isles the minister met McTavish by the bus stop early on a Sunday morning. With concern, he asked:

'Surely McTavish, you don't take the bus on the Sabbath day?'

'I'm sorry minister, but it's the only way I can get tae the harbour tae protest aboot the ferries runnin' on Sundays!'

*

Newsflash: After last night's game between England and Scotland, 10,000 beer cans were left in Trafalgar Square by Scottish football fans. Both of them have been arrested.

*

Jamesie stood in the dock with both arms in plaster.

'Do you mean to say that a man with two broken arms could give you that black eye?' asked the magistrate to Jamesie's complaining wife.

'Aye,' she replied, 'but he didnae have the broken arms till *after* he gie me the black eye.'

*

In a gentrified quarter of Edinburgh, Callum and Fergus were boasting in the pub about how much their houses had gone up in value.

'Mine's worth at least four hundred thousand now,' said Fergus.

'I'd get half a million for mine,' boasted Callum.

Wanting to include the regulars in his conversation, Fergus turned to the man next to him.

'I say there, what would you get if you sold your house?'

Jamesie looked up from his pint in disgust.

'Aboot six months in jail. Ah'm frae the council estate.'

*

Scots love the summer. For most of them, it's their favourite day of the year.

*

McTavish's wife died and he decided to put a notice in the local paper.

'Whit would you like it tae say?' asked the newspaper man.

McTavish was a bit worried about the cost so he said:

'Ah'm a man o' simple sentiment. I'll have no need for anything fancy. Just put 'Jeannie McTavish dead' and that'll dae.'

'Ye know ye there's a minimum charge for this – ye can have up tae three words more for the same price?'

McTavish thought for a moment.

'In that case, put: "Jeannie McTavish dead. Toyota for sale."'

*

Newsflash: A man who threw a coin on the pitch during a Glasgow Rangers match was arrested shortly afterwards. The police just followed the elastic band it was attached to.

*

An Englishman, an Irishman, and a Scotsman walked into a pub and each bought a pint of beer. Just as they were about to enjoy their drinks, a fly landed in each of their pints.

The Englishman pushed his beer away from him in disgust.

The Irishman fished the offending fly out of his beer and continued drinking it as if nothing had happened.

The Scotsman picked the fly out of his drink, held it out over the beer and then started yelling: 'SPIT IT OOT!'

*

Advert in the Aberdonian Times: 'Lost, a £5 note. Sentimental value.'

*

McNab phoned the dentist to enquire about the cost for a tooth extraction.

'85 pounds for an extraction, sir' the dentist replied.

'85 quid! Huv ye no' got anythin' cheaper?'

'That's the normal charge,' said the dentist.

'Whit aboot if ye didnae use any anaesthetic?'

'That's unusual, sir, but I could do it and would knock 15 pounds off.'

'Whit aboot if ye used one of your trainees and still without any anaesthetic?'

'I can't guarantee the work, and it'll be painful. But the price could drop by 20 pounds.'

'How aboot if ye make it a trainin' session, and ye had yer student do the extraction with the other students watchin' and learnin'?'

'It'll be good for the students', reflected the dentist. 'I'll charge you 5 pounds but it will be traumatic.'

'Och, that's better – it's a deal,' said McNab. 'Can ye confirm an appointment for the wife next Tuesday then?'

*

What do you call a Scottish Jew?

Rabbi Burns.

*

McTavish went on holiday to Canada.

Sitting in a bar, he noticed a huge stuffed animal on the wall with large antlers.

He asked the barman, 'What d'ye call that?'

The barman said 'That – why that's just a moose.'

'Jings!' exclaimed McTavish. 'I'd hate to see how big the cats are!'

*

A recent study conducted by Glasgow University found that the average Scotsman walks about 900 miles a year.

Another study by the Scottish Medical Association found that Scotsmen drink, on average, 22 gallons of alcohol a year.

This means, on average, Scotsmen get about 41 miles to the gallon.

Kind of makes you proud to be Scottish!

*

'Did you enjoy yer holiday at Saltcoats?'

'Aye.'

'And did ye have good weather?'

'Aye, but I missed it – I was in the bathroom at the time.'

*

Two Scottish ducks were flying along. One turns and says, 'Quack quack.'

The other turns around and says, 'A'm goin as quack as ah can!'

*

In Scotland there are only two seasons. Winter, and July.

*

A Scots minister was testing the children in his church to see if they understood the concept of getting to heaven. He asked them, 'If I sold my house and my car, had a big jumble sale and gave all my money to the church, would that get me into heaven?'

'NO!' the children answered.

'If I cleaned the church every day, looked after the grounds, and repainted the walls, would that get me into heaven?'

Again, the answer was 'No!'

'Well, then, persisted the minister, 'if I was kind to animals and gave sweeties to all the children, and loved my family, would that get me into heaven?'

Again, they all answered 'No!'

The clergyman continued, 'Then how CAN I get into heaven?'

A six year-old boy shouted out – 'Ye've got tae be deid first!'

*

In a Scottish classroom, the teacher asked a pupil:

'If you have 5 pounds, and I ask you to borrow 2, how many pounds do you have left?'

'5.'

*

Old McPherson, who had lost all his teeth, had a visit from the minister who noted that Tam had a bowl of almonds. 'My son gave me those, but I don't want them, you can have them' said McPherson.

The minister tucked into them and then said 'That was a funny present to give a man with no teeth.'

To which McPherson replied: 'Not really, they had chocolate on them...'

*

Callum decided to call his father-in-law 'The Exorcist' because every time he came to visit he made the spirits disappear...

*

'Why are ye drinking whisky through that lang straw, McTavish?'

'The doctor's telt me to keep away frae the bottle.'

*

Sandy's nephew came to him for advice.

'I have my choice of two women,' he said, 'a beautiful, penniless young girl who I love dearly, and a rich old widow who I can't stand.'

'Follow your heart; marry the girl you love,' advised Sandy.

'Very well, Uncle Sandy,' said the nephew, 'that's sound advice.'

'By the way,' asked Sandy, 'where does the widow live?'

*

'I hear Morag and yourself settled your difficulties and decided to get married after all,' Donald said to Angus.

'That's right,' said Angus, 'Morag's put on so much weight that we couldn't get the engagement ring off her finger.'

*

A Scotsman took a girl for a ride in a taxi. She was so beautiful he could hardly keep his eye on the meter.

*

Jamesie was traveling by train seated next to a stern-faced clergyman. As Jamesie pulled out a bottle of whisky from his pocket the clergyman glared and said reprovingly,

'Look here, I am sixty-five and I have never tasted whisky in my life!'

'Dinna worry, minister,' smiled Jamesie, pouring himself a dram. 'There's no risk of you starting now!'

*

Jamesie returned home from the pub the worse for wear.

He sat down on a bus next to a priest. His tie was stained, his face was plastered with red lipstick, and a half empty bottle of whisky was sticking out of his torn coat pocket. He opened his *Daily Record* and began reading. Then he asked the priest,

'Father, what causes arthritis?'

'Well my son, it's the result of loose living, being with cheap, wicked women, too much whisky and a contempt for your fellow man.'

'Well I'll be damned!' Jamesie muttered, returning to his paper.

The priest, feeling a little guilty, said, 'I'm very sorry. I didn't mean to upset you. How long have you had arthritis?'

'I don't, Father. But I was just reading here that the Pope does.'

*

Sandy was drinking at a pub all night. When he got up to leave, he fell flat on his face. He tried to stand again, but to no avail, falling flat on his face. He decided to crawl outside and get some fresh air to see whether that would sober him up. Once outside, he stood up and, sure enough, fell flat on his face. Being a tough Scot, he crawled all the way home.

When he got to the door, he stood up yet again, but fell flat on his face. He crawled through the door into his bedroom. When he reached his bed, he tried once more to stand upright. This time he managed to pull himself to his feet but fell into bed. He was sound asleep as soon as his head hit the pillow.

He woke the next morning to his wife shaking him and shouting,

'So, ye've been oot drinkin' as usual!'

'How do ye know that?' he complained innocently.

'Because the pub called tae say ye left yer wheelchair there again!'

*

A Scotsman was arguing with ticket collector as to whether the fare was £4.95 or £5.00. Finally the disgusted collector picked up the Scotsman's suitcase and hurled it off the train, just as they passed over a bridge. The suitcase landed with a splash.

'Mon!' screamed the Scotsman, 'isn't it enough that you try to overcharge me, but now you've tried to drown my only son!'

*

Why do bagpipers walk when they play?

To get away from the noise.

*

What's the definition of a gentleman?

Someone who knows how to play the bagpipes, but doesn't.

*

On the way to a football match at Wembley between England and Scotland, five Englishmen boarded a train just behind five Scots, who, as a group had only purchased one ticket.

Just before the ticket inspector came through, all the Scots piled into one of the lavatories at the end of the carriage. As the inspector passed the door, he knocked and called 'Tickets, please!'

One of the Scots slid a ticket under the door. It was punched, pushed back under the door, and when it was safe all the Scots came out and took their seats.

The Englishmen were tremendously impressed by the Scots' ingenuity. On the trip back, the five Englishmen decided to try this themselves and purchased only one ticket. They noticed that, oddly, the Scots had not purchased any tickets this time.

Again, just before the inspector came through, the Scots piled into one of lavatories, and the Englishmen into the one on the other side. Then one of the Scots came out, knocked on the Englishmen's stall and called 'Ticket, please!'

When the ticket slid out under the door, he picked it up and quickly went back to join his friends.

*

How many Edinburghians does it take to change a lightbulb?

Just one – to hold the lightbulb and then to expect the world to revolve around him.

*

An Englishman and Scotsman had a head on traffic collision on a lonely mountain road. To their amazement, neither was hurt, though their cars were badly damaged. In celebration of their luck, the Scotsman took a bottle of 12 year old single malt from his car and offered a swig to the Englishman, who took a large gulp gladly.

'Have another,' said the Scotsman. 'Ye've had a bad shock.'

The Englishman took a big swig and then offered the bottle to the Scotsman.

'No thanks,' he replied. 'I think I'll just sit here and wait for the police to arrive.'

*

A tourist from the American 'Bible Belt' went to morning service at a Presbyterian church in the Western Isles. It was soon evident that he was accustomed to a less formal atmosphere during worship, and from time to time interrupted the sermon and prayers by loudly exclaiming 'Praise the Lord!'

This went on for some time until an old Elder tapped the man on the shoulder and said sternly, 'We dinnae praise the Lord here!'

*

McNab was getting ready to go to the pub. He turned to his wife before leaving and said,

'Morag - put your hat and coat on lassie.'

'Aw, that's nice - are you taking me fer a drink?'

'Nah, just switching the central heating off while I'm oot.'

*

Caller to Directory Enquiries: 'I want a knitwear company in Woven.'

Operator: 'Woven? I've got no town of that name listed. Are you sure?

Caller: 'Yes, That's what it says on the label. "Woven in Scotland".'

*

McTavish broke the habit of a lifetime and bought two tickets for a raffle. One of his tickets won a 1,000 pound prize. He was asked how he felt about his big win.

'Disappointed' said McTavish. 'My other ticket didn't win anything.'

*

McDougal walked into a fish and chip shop. 'I want 10 pence worth of chips, please. I want lots of salt and vinegar on them and two pence worth of pickled onions. And wrap the whole lot in today's newspaper'.

*

In disgust at the cheap jibes in the paper about Scotsman, McNab wrote in an angry letter to the *Daily Telegraph*: 'If you print any more jokes about mean Scotsmen I shall stop borrowing your paper.'

*

How many Glaswegians does it take to change a lightbulb?

None. Glasgow looks better in the dark.

*

As a Christmas present one year, the Laird gave his gamekeeper, MacPhail, a deerstalker hat with ear-flaps. MacPhail was most appreciative and always wore it with the flaps tied under his chin to keep his ears warm in the winter winds. One cold, windy day the Laird noticed he was not wearing the hat.

'Where's the hat?' asked the Laird.

'I've given up wearing it since the accident,' replied MacPhail.

'Accident? I didn't know you'd had an accident.'

'Yes. A man offered me a nip of whisky and I had the earflaps down and never heard him.'

*

A Scottish prayer - 'Oh Lord, we do not ask you to give us wealth. But show us where it is!'

*

A Highland bus company changed its fares so that passengers could get six journeys instead of four for a pound. McNab was still unhappy.

'Whit good'll it do me,' he declared. 'Now I've got to walk to town six times instead of four to save a poond!'

*

Did you hear about the Scotsman who got caught making nuisance telephone calls? He kept reversing the charges.

*

McTavish went a bit deaf but he didn't want to pay for a hearing aid. So he bought a piece of flex, put one end in his top pocket and the other end in his ear. It didn't help his hearing but he found that people spoke to him more loudly.

*

Sandy took his girlfriend out for the evening. They returned to her flat just before midnight and as she kissed him goodnight she said:

'Be careful on your way home. I'd hate anyone to rob you of all the money you've saved this evening.'

*

'Donald suggested a candlelit dinner last night,' Shona reported to her friend the next day.

'That was dead romantic,' said her friend.

'Not really. It just saved him having to fix the fuse.'

*

Notice in the kirk magazine: 'If members of the congregation must put buttons in the collection, please provide your own buttons. Stop pulling them off the seat cushions.'

*

A Scotsman decided to get married so one morning he sent messages to three of his girlfriends, proposing marriage. Two phoned immediately to say 'yes' while the third phoned that night to say the same. He married the third girl saying, 'The lassie for me is the one who waits for the cheap rates.'

*

Sign on a Scottish golf course: 'Members must refrain from picking up lost balls until they have stopped rolling.'

*

A Scots chemistry teacher was giving a demonstration to his pupils. He dropped a pound coin into a beaker of acid and asked:

'Now class, will this coin be dissolved by the acid?'

One pupil put his hand up. 'No sir, it definitely will not!'

The teacher smiled. 'That's right, lad - well done! Now, can you explain why?'

The boy smiled back, 'Well, if the acid was going to dissolve your coin, you would have used a penny.'

*

In England, they will take a tree, cut it down, remove the branches and the bark until they are left with a cylinder. Next, they will take the cylinder of wood and turn it on a lathe and whittle away until they are left with a perfectly formed bat. The bat will be cured and treated to strengthen it and then, when it is finally ready, they will use it to knock a leather ball around a park.

In Scotland, they just throw the tree.

*

An Englishman met a Scotsman in the pub and said to him 'I will give you £100 if you can hold a one minute conversation with me, without mentioning any body part. If you do mention one then you have to give me the £100. Starting from now, OK?'

'Aye.'

*

The sleeper from London to Inverness stopped at a tiny Highland station, just as the sun was rising. A Londoner stepped off onto the platform, breathed in the pure, fresh air and turned to the old porter on the platform.

'Invigorating, isn't it?' said the Londoner.

'No,' said the old man. 'Inverurie.'

*

'Jamesie, huv ye heard the news?'

'Whit's that?'

'They're makin' one o' thae zombie horror films right here in Glesga – and they're payin' fae local people tae play the extras – I'm in, are you?'

'Aye, count me in – I bet we'll look guid in oor blood stained rags, staggering aboot the place an' moanin'.'

'Aye, but at some point we'll have tae sober up and get intae costume.'

*

An Englishman's car broke down in the Highlands. He called for assistance, and eventually a man in a van pulled up.

Are you a mechanic?' asked the Englishman.

'No,' he replied. 'I'm a McAllister.'

*

Newsflash: Scottish police have come up with a novel method to identify fans who throw coins on the pitch during football matches. They just wait for the end of the game and catch them when they sneak onto the pitch to get them back.

*

The minister was sharing a rail compartment with a Scot the worse for drink, who insisted on talking.

'Please don't speak to me,' said the minister. 'You're drunk.'

'Drunk?' replied the Scot. 'You're worse than me — you've got your collar on back to front.'

*

Said the Englishman to the boastful Scot: 'Take away your mountains, glens and lochs, and what have you got?'

'England,' replied the Scot.

*

It was cold on the upper deck and. the captain was concerned for the comfort of his passengers.
He called down: 'Is there a mackintosh down there big enough to keep two young lassies warm?'

'No, skipper,' came the reply, 'but there's a MacPherson willing to try.'

*

It had been a terrible winter with months of blizzards. McTavish hadn't been seen in the village for weeks, so a Red Cross rescue team struggled to his remote croft at the head of the glen. It was completely buried — only the chimney was showing.

'McTavish,' they shouted down the chimney. 'Are you there?'

'Wha's that?' came the answer.

'It's the Red Cross,' they called.

'Go away,' shouted McTavish. 'I made a donation last year!'

*

Newsflash: Parts of Glasgow are being transformed into war-torn ruins for a new Hollywood blockbuster. They have a special effects budget of nearly £2.50.

*

A farmer's wife offered her shepherd a drink. As she handed him his glass, she said it was extra good whisky, being fourteen years old. 'Weel, mistress,' said the shepherd regarding his glass sorrowfully, 'It's very small for its age.'

*

Newsflash: Government cutbacks are really starting to affect Glasgow General Hospital. The only heart and lung machine left is the haggis grinder in the kitchen.

*

McNab got a job at a sewage works. It was a warm day, so he took off his jacket and draped it over a handrail. Soon afterwards it slipped off the rail into the raw sewage.

He was just about to dive in when the boss shouted 'It's nae guid tae do that, the jacket's ruined!'

McNab shouted back. 'Aye, ah ken, but ma sandwiches are in the pocket.'

*

A Scots pessimist is a man who feels badly when he feels good for fear he'll feel worse when he feels better.

*

What do you call a Scottish parrot?

A Macaw.

*

McTavish was travelling by train from Edinburgh to London so he went to the train station and carefully handed over money for his ticket. The ticket clerk handed him the ticket and said, 'by the way, change at York.'

'I'll tak' it now, if you don't mind,' said McTavish.

*

Newsflash: Three Scotsmen have been murdered while wearing kilts. Police are beginning to see a pattern.

*

Did you hear about the man who gave up making haggis?

He didn't have the guts for it anymore.

*

A Govan wifie went into a posh dry cleaning shop in Bearsden and said to the shop owner, 'Can I sit down for a wee while, I've just had a bairn.'

The shop owner replied, 'I'm sorry, we can't repair scorched clothing.'

*

It was a bitterly cold day on the golf course and the caddy was expecting a large tip from his rich Scottish client. As they neared the clubhouse, the caddy heard the words he was longing to hear, 'This is for a hot toddy.' He held out his hand and a sugar cube was placed in it.

*

What do you call a skeleton in a kilt?

Boney Prince Charlie.

*

My wife was the last of five Scottish sisters to marry. The confetti was filthy.

*

Hamish was taking his girlfriend for a ride on his motorbike. As they passed a chip shop she sighed.

'My, those chips smell awfy nice.'

'Hold on a moment,' said Hamish with great gallantry. 'I'll drive a little closer so you can get a better smell.'

*

The minister was speaking to his wife after service on Sunday night.

'The service went well,' observed his wife.

'Aye, good attendance - and a tourist was present, but I did not see him.'

'But how do you know? '

'There was a five pound note in the collection box.'

*

Newsflash: With heavy snow on the way, Glasgow city council has been preparing by stockpiling salt. The chip shops must not be allowed to run out again.

*

Then there was the impatient Glasgow bus conductor who used to confuse his passengers by shouting 'come on, get off!'

*

Two negatives make a positive but only in Scotland do two positives make a negative - 'Aye right.'

*

'Ach, Donald, I can never drink tea the way I like it these days,' said Angus to his friend.

'Why's that?'

'Well,' observed Donald, 'I like it with two lumps of sugar, but if I drink it at home, I'll only take one lump, and if I drink it when I'm visiting, I always take three.'

*

Newsflash: A twelfth century sixpence has been uncovered at an archaeological dig in Aberdeen. Also found in the vicinity were four skeletons on their hands and knees.

*

The MacTavish brothers decided that one of their number would go to America and make his fortune, coming back to share with the rest of them. The youngest, Donald, was chosen for this task. Off he went, and he worked hard in America, and earned himself a fortune over a few years, and wrote to his brothers that he'd be returning with it. When he came back to Scotland he got off the boat, and looked around for his brothers, but could not see anyone who looked familiar. Finally, a group of bearded strangers approached.

'Ho, Donald, are ye not knowing yer own brothers?' asked the first one. Then Donald realised his brothers had grown beards.

'Fer heaven's sake, laddies, what would ye be growin' thae beards for, now?' he asked.

'We had to, lad, ye took the razor wi' ye!'

*

Newsflash: A taxi crashed into a lamp post in Aberdeen last night. Sixteen passengers were treated for injuries.

*

'How's yer new minister, McTavish?' said McDonald to the canny Highland villager.

'Aye, he's right enough, but I preferred the one before him.'

'Was he a better preacher?' asked McDonald.

'Naw', replied McTavish.

'Was he a better singer of the psalms then?'

'No, it was not that.'

'What then?'

'His auld clothes fitted me better.'

*

'It never rains but it pours.' I'm not a pessimist, I'm just Scottish.

*

Newsflash: A new technological development has now enabled large numbers of Scotsmen to work from home – Wetherspoon's has installed free wifi in all its pubs.

*

Why did McTavish join the Free Church?

He thought it was the only one where you didn't have to pay anything.

*

'If I am elected next week, I shall go from Holyrood to govern,' announced a politician at an election rally in Glasgow.

'So whit?' said a voice from the back of the hall. 'Ah'm goin tae Govan this efternoon!'

*

Many years ago a minister was being shaved by a barber who was the worse for drink. After the man had cut him three times, the minister proclaimed:

'The drink has a terrible effect, has it not?'

'Indeed sir,' said the barber with a wink. 'It makes the skin mair tender.'

*

'Do you not know where drunkards go, man?' asked the fire-breathing minister to a villager with a fondness for the bottle.

'Generally whaur the whisky's cheapesht,' came the reply.

*

A stuntman got a job with a film company based in Govan, but he had a terrible first day. He was set on fire, then he was thrown through a plate glass window, then finally he was run over by a car. After all that, when he finally arrived at work, he found the studios were closed!

*

Glasgow courtship ritual:

'Are you dancin'?'

'Are you askin'?'

'Well if you're dancing, I'm askin'!'

*

A portly Englishman was complaining about the food in a Scottish hotel.

'Mince, kale, and potatoes? In England that's food for pigs.'

'Then help yourself to a wee bit more,' said the waiter.

*

American tourist (to farmer): 'Say, if we climb this mountain, how far will we be able to see? Edinburgh?

'Och, further than that. '

'London?'

'Och, awfy further than that.'

'Not Europe, surely?'

'Och, further than that, even!'

'Say, look mister, just because we're Americans there's no need to make fun of us. Just how can we see further than Europe from the top of that mountain?'

The farmer smiled and replied: 'Weel, by the time ye've climbed tae the top, ye'll be able to see tae the moon!'

*

McDougal was on his deathbed. As his family gathered around him, he called out to his family in a trembling voice.

'Are ye here, wife?'

'I'm here, husband.'

'Are ye here, son?'

'I'm here, father.'

'Are ye here, daughter?'

'I'm here, father.'

McDougal sat up with a horrified expression on his face.

'Then who the hell's lookin' after the shop?'

*

How does a Scotsman greet his guests?

'You'll have had yer dinner.'

*

McTavish was on his deathbed.

'Jeannie,' he whispered faintly.

'Yes dear?' asked his wife by the bedside.

'Jeannie, could ye do one last thing fer me?'

'Anything, dear,' said his wife.

'Could I have just a wee bit of that ham on the table there?'

'Well, best not to.'

'It canna do me any harm now, lassie,' came the faint reply.

'Well no, but I was savin' it for after the funeral.'

*

'I hear McDougal left over a hundred thousand pounds when he died,' remarked McNab.

'McDougal didn't leave that money,' said McTavish, 'he was taken from it.'

*

Did you hear about the Scotsman who wanted to give to charity anonymously?

He always left his cheques unsigned.

*

Newsflash: Recent historical research has revealed why Scotsmen wear kilts. In 1317 Sandy McNab won a lady's tartan skirt in a raffle.

*

Two English pickpockets went into a Glasgow pub in search of money. A fierce struggle ensued.

'We didn't do so bad,' said one of them afterwards. 'We came out with twenty pounds.'

'But we had fifty when we went in,' complained the other.

*

Young Sandy had been out for the evening with his best girl. When he arrived home he found his father sitting up waiting for him. The old man looked up and shook his head.

'Have you been out with that girl again?' he asked.

'Yes, dad,' replied young Sandy. 'Why do you look so worried? '

'I was just wondering how much the evening cost.'

'No more than five pounds, dad.'

'Well, that wasn't too bad.'

'It was all she had,' said Sandy.

*

Donald and his brother Sandy were running the ferry service to Jura. One day it was very stormy and the boat tossed about violently on the giant waves.

'We'll sink, we'll sink!' wailed Donald.

'Quick, then, collect the fares,' shouted Sandy. 'Otherwise we will all be drooned afore they've paid.'

*

Mrs MacGregor was very ill. The only light in the room, coming from a tiny candle, showed the pallor of her white complexion.

'I don't think I'll make it through the night,' she said to her husband.

'I've got tae get back tae work,' he replied, 'but if you feel yourself slipping away, be sure to blow oot the candle.'

*

'That man cheats,' cried McNab as he entered the clubhouse. 'He lost his ball in the rough and played another ball without losing a stroke.'

'How do you know he didn't find it?' asked a friend.

'Because I've got it in my pocket.' replied McNab.

*

'I was pleased to see you at the kirk on Sunday, Jamesie,' said the minister.

'Och is that where I was?' he replied. 'I couldn't remember where on earth I went to after I left the pub.'

*

'How did you get that black eye, Sandy?'

'Shopping.'

'Shopping – how so?'

'All I did was ask the shopgirl how much she'd take off for cash!'

*

The police found McNab drunk in London, wearing full highland costume.

'Name?' asked the constable.

'McNab,' came the reply in a slurred voice. The policeman looked at his clothing suspiciously.

'Address?'

'I'll have ye know it'sh called a kilt, no a dress!'

*

Jamesie walked into an antiques shop and said:

'How much for thae set of antlers?'

'Two hundred poond,' said the shop owner.

'That's affa dear,' said Jamesie.

*

How was copper wire invented?

Two Scotsmen were arguing over a penny.

*

'Ah, Jeannie, drinking makes you look so bonnie.'

'But Donald, I dinnae drink!'

'But I do!'

*

'McDougall's dead. He fell into a vat of whisky.'

'What a shame. Was it a quick death?'

'I don't think so. He came oot twice to go to the lavvy!

*

McNab went into a shop to buy a pocket knife.

'Here's the very thing,' said the shopkeeper, 'four blades and a corkscrew.'

'Tell me,' said McNab, 'you havnae got one with four corkscrews and a blade have ye?'

*

'I hear you're a great believer in free speech.'

'I am that, Angus.'

'Well, do you mind if I use your phone?'

*

An Englishman and a Scotsman were stranded on a desert island after a plane crash. Their clothes were in rags and their food was running out.

'Chin up, old boy. I suppose it could always be worse,' said the Englishman.

'Oh, aye, it could,' agreed the Scotsman. 'I might have bought a return ticket.'

What do you call a Scotswoman with one leg?

Eileen.

'It's a terrible thing, is the drink,' said Sandy, handing his friend a glass of heavily diluted whisky. 'They say there's death in every glass.'

'Aye,'said Donald, looking at the contents, 'and I think this one was from drooning.'

What's the difference between Bing Crosby and Walt Disney?

Bing sings, but Walt Disney.

'My wife came to me on her hands and knees last night,' said Jamesie.

'Oh! What did she say?' replied Shuggie.

'"Come oot from under the bed and discuss this like a man."'

McTavish was en route to America with his family for their annual holiday.

'Are we nearly there yet?' whined one of the wee McNabs for the umpteenth time.

McTavish turned round angrily. 'Shut up and keep rowing!'

While staying at a country hotel, McNab noticed with disappointment the tiny pots of honey on the breakfast table. When the landlady came into the room, McNab pointed to one and said:

'I see ye keep a bee!'

*

A bagpiper was asked by a funeral director to play at a graveside service for an old Scots soldier who'd died without any family or friends left. The burial was to be at a remote spot in the Highlands.

The piper got lost and finally arrived an hour late at where he thought the service was. There was only a pile of earth, some shovels and two workmen having a smoke.

Embarrassed at being so late, and not wanting to let the old man down, the piper started to play a mournful lament over the grave.

The workmen put out their cigarettes and gathered around. The piper poured out his soul into the music, and as he played *Flower of Scotland*, the workers began to weep.

When he'd finished, the piper packed up his pipes and went back to his car. On the way he overheard one of the workers say:

'I've never seen anything like that before and I've been putting in septic tanks for twenty years.'

Also available for Amazon Kindle from Montpelier Publishing:

After Dinner Laughs: Jokes and Funny Stories for Speechmakers

Dr Smith: 'How's your new receptionist?'

Dr Jones: 'Highly efficient. I haven't seen a patient all week!'

This book is packed with clean quick-fire jokes and longer funny stories about all the usual suspects: bankers, lawyers, doctors, estate agents, Scotsmen, Irishmen, vicars, builders, mothers-in-law and many more. If you're hunting for jokes for a speech, public address, sermon or lecture or just looking for laughs, *After Dinner Laughs* will keep you chuckling, page after page.

The Bumper Book of Riddles, Puzzles and Rhymes

This book contains almost 300 brainteasers compiled in one big value volume.

The book features short riddles, long riddles, rhyming riddles, plus brainteasers and puzzles based on wordplay, arithmetic, puns and lateral thinking.

Why is a dead hen better than a live one? What is the difference between the Prince of Wales and a tennis ball? What can you keep even after giving it to someone else? Find out the answers to all these and more in this big book of family fun!

Wedding Jokes: Hilarious Gags for your Best Man's Speech

'My wife and I have agreed never to go to bed angry with one another. So far we've been up for three weeks...'

'My wife and I always compromise, I admit I'm wrong and she agrees with me...'

Whether you're making a speech for a wedding or an anniversary, or just want a good laugh, this laugh-a-minute book will keep you chortling at the ups and downs of weddings and married life.